D0177674

①

The support and assistance of the Advisory Committee on Women's Affairs, the Mental Health Foundation and Kidsarus II is gratefully acknowledged.

First published in Great Britain in 1987
by Hutchinson Children's Books
An imprint of Century Hutchinson Ltd
Brookmount House, 62-65 Chandos Place,
Covent Garden, London WC2N 4NW

Century Hutchinson Australia (Pty) Ltd
16-22 Church Street, Hawthorn, Melbourne, Victoria 3122

Century Hutchinson New Zealand Limited
32-34 View Road, PO Box 40-086, Glenfield, Auckland 10

Century Hutchinson South Africa (Pty) Ltd
PO Box 337, Bergvlei 2012, South Africa

Printed and bound in Hong Kong

ISBN 0 09 173536 X

What's Wrong with Bottoms?

by Jenny Hessell
Illustrated by Mandy Nelson

Hutchinson

London Melbourne Auckland Johannesburg

My Uncle Henry has a problem
with his bottom.

He keeps showing it to everyone.

Well, not everyone,
but he keeps showing it to me.

Uncle Henry came to live with us
when I was little.

We've always got on really well.

When I was smaller,
he used to carry me around on his shoulders
and he often bought presents
just for me.

He was my special friend.

But one day, he did something strange.

We were in his room and he unzipped his trousers.

He asked if I wanted to look at his penis.

I thought it was a silly thing for a man to do,
but I didn't like to say so.

'Don't tell your Mum,' said Uncle Henry.

I thought that was even sillier,
but he made me promise,
and I don't like to break promises.

Another day, he asked if he could put
his hand down my pants.

This was taking things too far.

'No fear,' I said,
and off I went to tell Mum.

Mum was very pleased I had told her.
But I could see that she was really cross
with Uncle Henry.

'Dad and I will talk to him about it tonight,'
she said. 'He's not allowed to do that.'

'I didn't think he was,' I answered,
'but I don't really understand why.
What's wrong with bottoms?'

Mum smiled.

'There's nothing wrong with bottoms.
But there are things to do with bottoms
which are okay and things
which aren't okay.

'Remember when Josh was little?' she said.
'He was always pulling down his pants
and showing off his bare bottom.

'He thought it was very funny
and so did everyone else.
We used to have a good laugh about it.

'And remember the time
you walked to the shops
wearing a sunhat and a pair of gumboots
and nothing else!

'Well, that was okay, too,
we even took a photo of you
coming home.

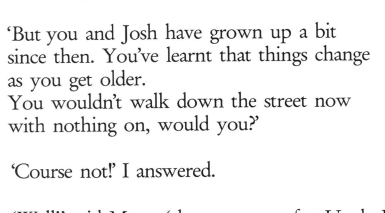

'But you and Josh have grown up a bit
since then. You've learnt that things change
as you get older.
You wouldn't walk down the street now
with nothing on, would you?'

'Course not!' I answered.

'Well!' said Mum, 'the same goes for Uncle Henry.
He knows very well
that he musn't go around
showing off his bottom to children
and asking them to do things
they don't like.'

'Perhaps he doesn't understand,' I said.

'Oh yes, he does!' said Mum.
'That's why he waited
till you were on your own.
He hasn't pulled down his pants
in the livingroom while we're all
watching TV, has he?'

'No,' I laughed. 'That's probably why he made me promise not to tell you.'

'That's right,' said Mum. 'And in some ways that's the worst part of it. Promises shouldn't be used for things like that — especially not by friends.'

I was glad I had told Mum.

But I was worried about what would happen
to Uncle Henry.

Later that evening, I followed Mum
into the baby's room.

Rosie was standing in her cot,
banging Teddy against the wall.

She smiled as we came in.

'What are you going to tell Uncle Henry?'
I asked.

'I'm going to tell him that there are some things
an adult mustn't ask a child to do,'
Mum said. 'And I'm going to tell him
that he can't stay here any more.'

I felt a bit sad when she said that.

'Does he *have* to go away?' I asked.

'Yes,' said Mum, 'because he needs help to change, and we can't give him that help.'

'I s'pose you're right,' I said.

Rosie was bouncing up and down
in her cot tugging at her nappy.

'Mummy,' she shouted. 'Poo!'

'Good grief! More bottoms,' I groaned.
'I think I've had enough for one day!'